ENCOURAGING NEW CHRISTIANS

Michael C. Griffiths

"Let us hold fast the confession of our hope without wavering, for he who promised is faithful; and let us consider how to stir up one another to love and good works, not neglecting to meet together, as is the habit of some, but encouraging one another, and all the more as you see the Day drawing near." Hebrews 10:23-25 (RSV)

InterVarsity Press is the book-publishing division of Inter-Varsity Christian Fellowship, a student movement active on campus at hundreds of universities, colleges and schools of nursing. For information about local and regional activities, write IVCF, 233 Langdon St., Madison, WI 53703.

Distributed in Canada through InterVarsity Press, 860 Denison St., Markham, Ontario L3R 4H1, Canada.

ISBN 0-87784-106-3

Printed in the United States of America

---

24 23 22 21 20 19 18 17
91 90 89 88

"I care for nobody, no, not I, and nobody cares for me," sang the Jolly Miller of Dee, but he had no cause to be half so blithe. A lark from any respectable nest would have reminded him of the care which older birds have for younger ones, and certainly such an irresponsible attitude as his is out of place among Christians. But there is a danger that our very proper emphasis on the necessity of individual conversion and personal devotion to Christ may lead to an unbalanced individualism, whereas the Bible uses several metaphors to show that the newly born-again person is a member of God's family, one stone among many stones in a building, or one member of a body (Eph 2:19-22; Rom 12:4-8; 1 Cor 12:12-31). To many people, however, the practical implications of this are not always obvious or even welcome. While we may not snarl with Cain "Am I my brother's keeper?" we like to feel that other people will mind their own business, and we will mind ours too. We may even feel that it is not quite right to be deeply interested in the religious life of others, and we may resent it when others probe too closely into the state of our own hearts.

Obviously we must have a deep respect for the sanctity of human personality, yet it is well to recognize that Scripture seems to have little place for Robinson Crusoe religion. The Bible urges us to "consider how to stir up one another to love and good works, not neglecting to meet together . . . but encouraging one another" (Heb 10:24-25).

Many of us require a bit of prodding and benefit tremendously by tactful, gracious, mutual "stirring up." The same writer tells us, "See to it that no one fail to obtain the grace of God; that no 'root of bitterness' spring up and cause trouble, and by it the many become defiled" (Heb 12:15-16). This shows we have a duty positively to help one another in the Christian life, and negatively to avoid anything which would hinder others. We are in fact our brother's keeper. Our indifference to our mutual responsibilities will mean that the whole body suffers through our default. We may liken ourselves to a team of mountaineers roped together; when one slips the rest of us hold fast until he has regained his footing. And again, if one of the party is careless or slow, he will delay all the rest.

This mutual responsibility has particular application to younger Christians and is especially important where recent converts are concerned. When Saul of Tarsus was converted, we are told that "a disciple," not apparently a man of outstanding prominence, named Ananias, was told by God to seek him out and welcome the young Christian into the fellowship as "brother Saul." Then we read that "for several days [Saul] was with the disciples at Damascus," and that they later helped him escape by letting him down from the wall in a basket. Going to Jerusalem, he is befriended by Barnabas, who introduces him to the disciples there. Later, when a church begins at Antioch, and Barnabas is put in charge, he seeks out Saul to help him in this work. From all this we see both that he was in the company of other Christians from his earliest days and also that certain individuals found that they were able to give him special friendship and encouragement.

The same is true today. A recent graduate writes as follows: "I enjoyed the sermons and Bible readings at ____________ tremendously, but what helped me most in my Christian life was the friendship of ____________. After I had known him a little while, he suggested that we might meet occasionally to read the Bible together. I jumped at the chance, having already admired his quiet, joyful witness to the power of Christ. Those weekly meetings became something to look forward to. I learned to read the Bible really purposefully and came to trust and love it.

"There were many difficulties about questions of doctrine and practice, but the natural thing seemed to be to ask ____________ and he usually had a sensible answer.

"More than what he said, however, it was what he was consistently, in every part of university life, which I believe had most influence in encouraging me to 'grow up into Christ in all things.' "

The purpose of this booklet is to give practical advice on ways of helping other young converts. We may have been used recently to bring someone to know Christ as Savior. Now our responsibility has really begun, for helping young Christians is at least as important, and certainly just as thrilling, as leading them to Christ. Or perhaps we know of someone who has just professed conversion as the result of some evangelistic meeting and realize that he or she needs help. We must make contact as soon as possible. Newborn babes must not be left on drafty doorsteps. Our approach will have to be tactful and even diffident, as we make it clear that, while we have no desire to pry into another person's life, we should like to help, if we may. In most cases our friendly offer will be willingly accepted.

How Can I Help?

By prayer. We may have prayed for our friends' conversion, but the proportion of Scripture would suggest that we have an even greater responsibility to pray for them now. It is interesting to notice that most New Testament prayers are in fact for young Christians and for their growth (see Eph 1:16-23; 3:14-21; Phil 1:9-11; 1 Thess 1:2; 3:10, and so on). We shall not go wrong if we seek for our friends (and for ourselves) those blessings which Paul sought for the young Christians for whom he felt responsible.

By friendship. Young converts need real Christian friendship. All of us, whether young or old in the faith, find that Christian friends are among the greatest of God's blessings and the means which he often uses to help us along. How frequently in the New Testament Christians are found working in pairs! Our Lord sent out his disciples two by two (Mk 6:7). We naturally link together the names of

Peter and John, Barnabas and Saul, Paul and Silas, Aquila and Priscilla. It is a serious thing if we fail the young Christian here. A man who had made a profession of conversion, and who at first attended Inter-Varsity meetings with regularity, nonetheless made disappointing progress. The reason was not hard to discover. He complained bitterly that none of the Christians in his college had really befriended him. They had all been too busy with their own concerns and their own friends, and no one had had time to spare for this lonely young Christian. The blame for the lack of progress was not his. There is no substitute for real friendship.

It will be a costly business. It will mean spending less time with older friends. It will mean disciplining ourselves with regard to special friendships with members of the other sex which can so easily take up too large a proportion of our time while we are still students. It will mean less time spent on selfish hobbies and pursuits in which others cannot take part. It will mean time and effort spent in going around to their rooms for a chat or in looking them up to see whether they will accompany us to some meeting that we know will be a help. We shall encourage them to call on us at odd times for a talk over coffee. And when new Christians drop in, we shall never be too busy, and will make it clear that we are glad to see them. There will always be time for a short prayer before they go. We shall seek common means of recreation (which may mean teaching, or being taught something new), or going out for a walk or bicycle ride into the surrounding country. It takes time and trouble to build a real friendship, one which is not a mere social acquaintance but a full human relationship.

But how worthwhile it will prove to be! Those words of cheerful and sympathetic encouragement at the right time, that discussion of some pressing problem in a humble rather than a dictatorial way, make all the difference. We shall find that we return to our ordinary tasks after the friend has gone warmed and encouraged ourselves by our fellowship together. Right through our Christian experience such friendship helps us on. "Iron sharpens iron, and one man sharpens another" (Prov 27:17). It is this mutual rubbing off of corners where each raises the standards of the other, that is one of its richest blessings.

As soon as possible we should introduce the new convert to our other Christian friends, for our friendship must not become exclusive or possessive. We shall rejoice as we see him or her getting to know them, and asking counsel from them too. Let us beware of making new Christians too dependent upon us or of turning them into little replicas of ourselves. Let their dependence be on Christ alone and encourage them to develop that mature sense of mutual responsibility which all Christians should have for one another. May the Christian circles in which we move be marked by real Christian friendships, enriching the experience of all.

By example. Our example influences every Christian with whom we come into contact, but especially is this true of young Christians. In the letter quoted earlier it was what the Christian friend *was,* more than what he said, which had the greater effect. Our new friends will watch our example and in the early days, at least, their lives as Christians will be modeled on ours. They will notice the way we talk, the way we allocate our time and money, the way we face difficulties, and indeed everything about us. Their earliest ideas about Christian living will be derived from us. If we are inconsistent, then we make it all the harder for them to live a consistent life. They will soon see through any false piety put on for their benefit.

It is a terrible thing when the growth of young Christians is hindered because of the low standards of the Christian group in which they move. All of us tend to live down to the lowest accepted standard, rather than reaching up to the highest, so that the whole fellowship may go on growing. We must point to the Lord Jesus, seeking to walk even as he walked, and remembering that God's destiny for us is that we should be conformed to the image of his Son. "Be imitators of me," says Paul, "as I am of Christ" (1 Cor 11:1). Let us live such a life ourselves, and urge our younger Christian friends to do the same. If later they outstrip us in the Christian race, then let us thankfully follow their lead in turn.

By letter writing. Paul was always writing letters to his Christian friends—and the postal services were by no means as efficient as they are now. When, after only three weeks at Thessalonica, he was separated from the young converts there, he prayed for them, wrote a letter, sent a friend to visit them and wanted to come himself. It happens not infrequently that someone is converted toward the end of a term or academic year, and the vacation may be a period of great difficulty for young Christians, especially if they return to an unsympathetic home or to unhelpful friendships and associations. They may feel very lost and alone. What a difference it makes to find a cheery letter waiting in the mailbox. Don't preach a long sermon; but put in something of help and encouragement. Remind them, perhaps, that this time of testing can become a time of blessing if they learn to depend on the Lord and not rely too much on Christian fellowship. But wherever possible they should be linked with an active fellowship at home. Perhaps, as Paul did, we can get some Christian friend to visit them. If we can invite them to our own home, so much the better, especially if we are privileged to have a real Christian home. But in any case we must do our utmost by letters and by visiting to keep our friends encouraged.

By lending books. Books are not much use on our shelves, except to look impressive. They are far better in the hands of someone who will read them. There will be some books, of course, that young Christians should be encouraged to possess for themselves right from the start. We might give them *Being a Christian* almost at once and *Christ in You* within a week or so. Later, as we look over a book table together, we can recommend others: "What, haven't you read that?" There are some books which we shall feel we must have available for lending. We might even use some of the money which we set apart for the Lord's work for the purchase of such titles. Obviously, we cannot buy everything. But we should make ourselves knowledgeable about books, so that we can recommend something, whatever the problem brought to us may be. Read reviews, discuss books with older Christian friends who are widely read, borrow books yourself and above all gradually build up your own library.

Be an enthusiast. Some people are so good at lending books that it is impossible to escape from their rooms without some book to read. We may feel that a tonic is required and prescribe a stirring biography such as those of Luther, Borden of Yale, Henry Martyn or Hudson Taylor. We may suggest something very practical and challenging like *The Cost of Commitment;* or, perhaps a solid diet is needed leading to a more thorough knowledge of Christian doctrine. For such we shall want to recommend *Basic Christianity* or *Knowing God.* We ourselves ought always to be reading something fresh and, by our example, inculcating this excellent habit from the very beginning of the new convert's Christian life.

What Must I Encourage?

A realization of what has happened. Our friends may still be very confused about just what happened to them when they became Christians. Probably it has been just one particular aspect of salvation which they have heard explained and which has resulted in their making a profession of conversion. We shall need to explain the whole gospel very simply all over again, so that they have a bird's-eye view, as it were, of all that God has revealed of his purposes for us. We may perhaps use the words of Romans 8 or Ephesians 1 to explain it to them, or by taking 2 Corinthians 13:14 as a summary, we can describe a Christian as one who has experienced:

(a) The grace of the Lord Jesus Christ. Explain how sinners are forgiven not for any merit of our own, but because Christ died for us and bore our sins, so that we might receive his righteousness. Show how repentance and faith are the means by which we appropriate what Christ did for us on the cross. (See Jn 3:14-20; Rom 3:21-26; 2 Cor 5:14-21; 8:9.)

(b) The love of God. Explain that we have now entered into a new relationship with God the Father. We have become children of God. As such, we enjoy such privileges as access to him in prayer. We also accept responsibilities, namely, to live like his children. (See Mt 6:25-34; 1 Jn 3:1-3.)

(c) The fellowship of the Holy Spirit. Explain the new birth and how Christ lives in us through his

Spirit, who makes the Lord Jesus real to us, helps us to pray and to understand the Bible, and who changes us into the likeness of the Lord Jesus. (See Jn 3:3-8; 16:7-15; Rom 8:1-17; 2 Cor 3:18.)

Young Christians should be taken regularly to evangelistic services in order that, by hearing the gospel preached, they may come to a deepened understanding of all the facets of the glory of God's grace, and see the gospel in all the fullness of its scriptural presentation, rather than being content with just that one aspect of it which they first appreciated.

A sense of assurance. Young Christians seldom fully understand the gospel. They may or may not have been very deeply stirred emotionally at the time of conversion. In either case we must make it quite plain that their new standing with God does not depend upon feelings but upon facts. Feelings will vary, faith may waver, but facts are unshakable. Let us remind them therefore that their assurance of salvation depends upon:

(a) The Word of God. Draw attention to some of the promises of Scripture (e.g., Jn 6:37; 10:28-29) and point out that God does not break his promises. His very character guarantees our salvation. God has spoken.

(b) The work of Christ. Point out that it is not a question of screwing up some faith, but rather of a simple, trustful dependence upon Christ and his finished work on the cross. Christ has died.

(c) The witness of the Spirit. He gives both an inward, subjective conviction (Rom 5:5; 8:16; 1 Jn 3:24) and an outward, objective evidence in that fruit of the Spirit which becomes manifest in the lives of true believers (Gal 5:22). The Spirit is working.

If our friends are worried about their assurance we can point out that this very concern is an evidence of the Spirit's work; that we ought to examine ourselves to see whether we are in the faith; and that this very anxiety will cast us more completely upon God. But if they are depressed we may have to point to some evidence of the Spirit's work—a new hunger for God, an increased sense of sinfulness or of conflict, a burning desire for holiness or a concern for others—which they may not have recognized. It is right for us to look for the fruit as evidence, but we should remind them that it is to be brought forth "with patience," and that it may develop slowly but surely. Nonetheless let us constantly urge one another that it is by our fruits that we are to be known and that a growing likeness to the Savior is the best evidence of the new birth.

This is the time also to warn new Christians (for example, from Heb 13) that they are sure to meet real tests and trials of faith sooner or later. Warn them that at the time it will seem very unpleasant, but that when they endure and triumph over them, they will yield the peaceable fruit of righteousness.

Daily Bible reading and prayer. Remember that very few people today have much Christian background and that a word from us on the absolute necessity of a "Quiet Time" or "Morning Watch" will probably not be much help unless we can give some idea of how to set about it. The best way to teach is by example. Therefore, offer to read and pray with new converts at regular intervals, perhaps after lunch or dinner together once a week or as frequently as they may feel necessary.

Introduce them to a Bible reading system. As soon as possible also encourage them to use *Grow Your Christian Life* with the object of leading them on eventually to *Search the Scriptures* or *This Morning with God* which takes the reader through the whole Bible in three to five years. This system of passages set for each day's reading with questions designed to draw out the meaning encourages students to digest what they read for themselves. Let us not hesitate when we meet in the morning to inquire occasionally about that morning's reading and what they have discovered in it. This keeps them (and us!) up to the mark and enables us to help with difficulties, or to explain obscurities.

When we meet to read together, it is a help to study some specific passage, preferably one which has some bearing on any problem they may be facing at the time. For example, we might choose 1 John 1:1—2:2 on forgiveness, or Hebrews 12:1-15 on endurance. We must make it interesting and thrilling. Teach them to divide it up and extract the chief lessons from it, to select a helpful verse and perhaps commit it to memory. Then we can suggest that we pray together briefly, so praying in the lessons we have learned, using the words of the passage itself. Let our prayer be natural in manner, scriptural in content, and short in duration. If we pray for half an hour they may be discouraged! Make a habit, of course, of praying at other times also, for example when we drop in to see each other or after discussing some special problem. After they have got used to praying with us, another person can join in, and soon our new friends will find that they are in a small prayer meeting and that it does not seem at all strange! But try to avoid the awkward situation where everyone prays around and all present feel that they must pray, whether they want to or not. For help in private prayer recommend the pamphlet *Quiet Time* as well as the relevant chapters of *The Fight*.

We must emphasize strongly the need for being unhurried, which will involve rising in good time before breakfast. One young Christian appeared to be making remarkable progress, outstripping others who had been Christians for a much longer period. Those who lived near knew the reason. Although first down to breakfast, he rose early enough to have over an hour of quiet beforehand, and then returned afterward for a further half-hour of Bible study before lectures. What a lesson to many of us who had been Christians so much longer! He loved meeting with his Lord much more than he loved lying in bed in the morning.

A consistent Christian life. New converts will almost certainly realize, now that they are Christians, that a new standard of life is called for. But they may find it very hard to break off the old ways of living and speaking and thinking. We shall be able to help here, especially when they give way to some temptation. They may have a great sense of failure, and feel that their Christian life has been ruined beyond repair. Then we shall point them to the scriptural teaching about this (e.g., 1 Jn 1:7—2:2) that the Christian ideal is sinlessness, but that if we sin, we may confess to the Lord and know that he is faithful and just to forgive us our sin. Never minimize sin, but always magnify grace. We must never allow ourselves to appear to be shocked, and never pull back our holy hems, if we possess them, or they will never come back to us for help again. Neither should we give the impression that we never have temptations, or that we never let the Lord down, but be ready to speak frankly of our own difficulties and failures, and to pray over them together. Remember that our example of a consistent life will do more than any amount of talk. Let us not be mere negativists either, but positive in showing Christian unselfishness and practical thoughtfulness.

There are certain things from which most evangelical Christians refrain or abstain, commonly termed "worldly" or "doubtful." But it is very important that we do not lay down rules not found in Scripture, however strongly we may feel about these things. We may explain biblical principles but we should not insist upon (or even mention) negative details. For example, we should ask, "Is it to the glory of God? Does it harm my spiritual life? Does it cause my brother to stumble?" rather than spend our time proclaiming "Thou shalt not smoke, drink, dance or play cards!" It is obviously far better that, when a person drops some habit or practice, it should be because they have come to the conclusion that it would be wrong for them, and not just because they are conforming to the customs of their particular Christian set.

To an older Christian who is neglecting some regular meeting of spiritual benefit in favor of some less worthy activity we may feel we ought to speak more clearly and specifically. But let us by all means be positive. Paul said that he travailed "until Christ be formed in you" (Gal 4:19). Let us make certain that we encourage others to go the whole way, and not fall short of this goal through a negative legalism.

A mature understanding. Young Christians should be encouraged to think for themselves. Don't stultify thought by giving them some ready-made system. At first some things may have to be accepted on trust; but, as we grow, each and every part of Christian doctrine needs to be thought through. "In thinking be mature," urges Paul (1 Cor 14:20). Young Christians are usually marked by a lack of discrimination and a readiness to accept any plausible-sounding theory without really testing to see whether it is scriptural. But we should never draw in a horrified breath and say "How dreadfully unsound!" Let there be no "sound barriers" between us! We want them to come to an understanding of the truth not for fear of being thought unsound but because they find from the Bible that these things are so.

Encourage them to read books that will help to sort out their ideas, avoiding a light diet of nothing but subjective, devotional literature, and giving time to a proportion of meaty, doctrinal books. We ought not to introduce difficulties before they arise naturally in their own mind, but let them be dealt with as they come along. Let us not be impatient, but rather remember how long it took us to sort out all these things. We shall seek to answer the problems raised but if one should defeat us we shall not be afraid to say so and to suggest that the answer should be sought from somebody else. If the problem is in a field which is not familiar to us—educational psychology, perhaps, or the relation between science and theology—then we shall introduce our friend to a Christian who works in such a field.

Encourage the development of discernment. A person must not accept something merely because it is in a book (whoever the publisher), or because it comes from a pulpit (whoever the preacher). How encouraging it is when a Christian says, "Yes, I enjoyed the sermon, until that last section, which seemed to conflict with the teaching of the Bible." Only as we learn to test all teaching by Scripture will we learn to distinguish between all the babel of false sects and spurious scholarship and the consistent tones of biblical truth.

Church membership. It is important that, if new converts are not already attending some local church, they should be encouraged to do so at once. It is quite wrong, as well as foolish, to go to Inter-Varsity or other meetings to the exclusion of fellowship in a local church. The time will soon come to leave the university and then they will spend the greater part of their lives as the members of such churches. If people already have some denominational loyalty, then we must not proselytize them for our own denomination, however excellent, but encourage them to attach themselves to some live church of their own denomination where the gospel is faithfully preached. If we can go with them, so much the better; or we can ask a keen Christian of their own denomination to accompany them instead. If the local churches in their home district lack a biblical ministry, it is sometimes difficult to know where to take young Christians. If they are growing in discernment, they will soon grow dissatisfied with unscriptural teaching. If they express this, then we may have to remind them that, later in life, they may not infrequently find themselves in this depressing kind of situation, and that rather than just criticizing, they will have to pray and work for the revival of the church and its ministry. But we must leave them to find their own solution; certainly they should not be encouraged to be constantly moving about changing their place of worship. It is important that we should learn to settle down in one local church, working loyally within it, without, of course, becoming a narrow denominationalist. It is also extremely important that young converts be encouraged to value the Lord's Supper and to make a point of regularly remembering the Lord in the way he commanded (1 Cor 11:24-26).

An active witness. If new converts are growing healthily, they will spontaneously begin to witness to their friends and want to win them for Christ. If not, we may have to encourage them in this by suggesting that they should invite particular non-Christian friends to some evangelistic meeting. Another method is to guide the conversation when some third person is present so that they are given the opportunity of bearing simple personal testimony to what the Lord has done.

It will be invaluable if, during summer vacation, they can be persuaded to go, preferably with us or someone they know, to one of the camps or programs organized by Inter-Varsity. These are wonderful opportunities for bringing shy souls out of their shells and launching them into a life of fearless witness. They may be shy or reluctant at first and wonder whether they are quite prepared for it; but very many young Christians have found great blessing in such ventures, as well as enjoying fellowship during a long period of absence from the warmth of the college group.

Regular giving. Sooner or later something needs to be said about giving. Paul had no hesitation in turning from the sublime marvels of the final resurrection to say "Now concerning the contribution . . ." (1 Cor 16:1), and instructed the young Christians to lay something aside on the first day of each week, according as God has prospered every one of them. Christians in our churches need to realize their responsibility to employ their money as belonging to the Lord. We can foster this in our universities by stressing the principle with each new convert.

A sense of vocation. All Christians ought to pray that the Lord will direct them into the place of his choosing both as regards profession and geographical location. We need to encourage young converts to adopt this new attitude towards the spending of their one precious life span so that they will want to use it in Christ's service. They need not feel that this necessarily means "full-time service" in the special sense in which this term is often used. But they must realize that we need to be full-time Christians in whatever employment the Lord may put us.

Paul, however, often seems to have around him a number of recent converts who were being trained for what we call "full-time service" (Acts 20:4), men who, faced with the need for missionaries, left all to serve Christ. Young converts in our universities ought also to face the same challenge. The principle must be grasped that, whatever means of gaining a livelihood they may adopt, they are missionaries for Christ in whatever city or village the Lord leads them to live and work.

Fellowship. If we do our job properly and help our new friends, then it will not be long before everybody has ceased to think of them as young Christians at all. They will have taken their full places in the Christian fellowship, experiencing that mutual comfort and exercising that mutual responsibility which is part of the life of every mature Christian. "We know that we have passed out of death into life, because we love the brethren" (1 Jn 3:14). The time should come when, rising from prayer, we catch in their eyes that love of the brethren. It is then that we know we are indeed fellow members of the family of God.

Love for the Lord. Very few people would seem to be converted for purely altruistic motives. So often the desire for salvation is basically selfish rather than God-glorifying. A desire to escape hell, to be delivered from a particular besetting sin or to become a better person in one's own estimation and in the eyes of other people is often a strong motive. The Lord himself seems to have allowed people to come on a basis of their need (Mt 11:28; 20:32; Jn 5:6, and others) and in his mercy he still does. But spiritual growth should result in a realization of such self-interested motives and growing love for the Lord himself. When the younger Christian is able to pray with Job "Though he slay me, yet will I trust in him" (Job 13:15 KJV), we may rejoice at this sign of a fuller surrender to him.

It is this utterly fundamental love for Christ which ensures that a man's or a woman's whole life purpose is to love and serve God to the utmost of one's heart, mind and strength. It is easy sometimes to lose sight of essentials in the externals of the

Christian faith, and to become too exclusively interested in church politics, theological controversy, prophecy or fiddling distinctions of one kind or another, while imperceptibly the spiritual life becomes a shrunken, dried-up, barren, unattractive thing. Only love for the Lord himself is a sure antidote for spiritual atrophy.

Conclusion

When the Alexandrian Jew Apollos came to Ephesus, he came as a man with great natural gifts, a good knowledge of the Scriptures and a desire to impart spiritual knowledge to others. Yet we read that his knowledge and his experience were defective. So a young Christian couple, Aquila and Priscilla, who as far as we can see, were converted only after Paul came to live with them in Corinth, "took him and expounded to him the way of God more accurately" (Acts 18:1-3, 24-28). And so when this man went on to Achaia, he went as an able gospel minister and a successful evangelist. All this was due indirectly to the wise pastoral work first of Paul, then of that insignificant Christian couple, who made tents for a living.

That young and immature Christian whom we seek to help, may become, like Apollos, a man or woman greatly used of God to the conversion and establishing of many. They may far surpass us in Christian usefulness and spiritual progress; and yet it has been our great privilege to be used of God to start them on the Christian way.

Let us then go out with a full heart to exhort and encourage one another, and especially to help one another to grow in grace and the knowledge of our Lord and Savior Jesus Christ. To him be the glory both now and for ever. Amen.

Michael C. Griffiths is principal of London Bible College and former director of the Overseas Missionary Fellowship.

Further reading from InterVarsity Press

Basic Christianity John R. W. Stott presents a clear statement of the fundamental content of Christianity. *142 pages, paper*

Quiet Time This guidebook suggests practical methods for a meaningful, daily communion with God. *30 pages, paper*

Grow Your Christian Life directs personal Bible study on topics such as personal evangelism, sin and growth, knowing God's will and Christian marriage. *84 studies, paper*

The Fight John White looks at the basics—prayer, Bible study, evangelism, faith, fellowship, work and guidance—offering refreshing insights into the struggles and joys of life in Christ. *230 pages, paper*

Knowing God J. I. Packer discloses the nature and character of God and how to get to know him, not only informing the mind but warming the heart and inspiring devotion. *256 pages, paper*

Out of the Saltshaker Rebecca M. Pippert writes a basic guide to evangelism as a natural way of life. *192 pages, paper*

Paths of Leadership Andrew T. Le Peau describes various discipling styles for those who want to help others grow in Christ. *126 pages, paper*

InterVarsity Press is only one aspect of the total ministry of Inter-Varsity Christian Fellowship. IVCF traces its spiritual foundations back to Cambridge University in 1877. Today more than 400 field staff members reach over 750 colleges and universities in the United States. The Nurses Christian Fellowship, a department of IVCF, has groups at more than 100 campuses and schools of nursing. The Student Missions Fellowship has 125 chapters in Bible colleges and other Christian schools. The Theological Students Fellowship, geared to students in seminaries and graduate departments of religious studies, comprises 30 groups nationwide.

The aim of students and faculty in IVCF is to present a strong evangelical witness on campus, to strengthen each other spiritually and to present the call of God to the foreign mission field. Each campus chapter is self-sustaining, self-governing and self-propagating.

To help students reach these goals, IVCF publishes, along with the Inter-Varsity Press titles, HIS, "the magazine of campus Christian living," and *The Nurses Lamp,* geared to the nursing profession. The multimedia branch of Inter-Varsity, TWENTYONEHUNDRED, produces several presentations which aid students and staff in evangelism, discipleship and missions awareness.

IVCF is also affiliated with the IFES (International Fellowship of Evangelical Students) which links together the student movements in over 90 countries around the world. The IFES also offers resources of people, money and materials to countries only just beginning their own indigenous movements.

For more information, write to IVCF, 233 Langdon, Madison, Wisconsin 53703.